Wave Rider

Poetic Journey from Abuse to Wholeness

Rebecca Pott Fitton

Terra Nova Books

SANTA FE, NEW MEXICO

Library of Congress Control Number 2016958550

Distributed by SCB Distributors (800) 729-6423

Published by Terra Nova Books, Santa Fe, New Mexico.
www.TerraNovaBooks.com

ISBN 978-1-938288-74-6

Wave Rider

*This book is dedicated to my friend
Paul K. Chitwood.*

Contents

Preface

Rainbow Aura. A rare and magnificent energy field representing a chosen incarnation for the "soul" purpose of spiritual enlightenment, while encouraging others on a similar journey. That was my first impression meeting Rebecca.

Living a spiritual life is never easy. Rebecca has faced great challenges, always choosing courage over fear. She inspires us to stay focused on our path by teaching us there is a reason and a purpose for every step along our journey. We watch her transformation from wounded bird to powerful warrior as she shares through her poems the intimate details of an extraordinary life. She gives us each a glimpse of the potential we all possess.

Rebecca is a teacher who challenges, an author who inspires and a warrior who transforms.

—Christine Celek Schmit

Acknowledgments and Gratitude

My interdisciplinary healing journey began in Cincinnati, Ohio. I am grateful for the wisdom and skills of these healers: Carole Poffinbarger, Christine Celek Schmit, Dorothy Shaffer, Edie Moore, Helen Yamada, Irene Giessl, Jean Shinoda Bolen, Lauren Artress, Mary Branch Grove, and Starhawk.

In Santa Fe, New Mexico, the disciplines and expertise expanded multidimensionally. I am grateful to the following healers and teachers for their incredible talents and steadfast support of my journey: Cathy Black, James Jereb, Jason Hao, Jeraldine Peterson-Mark, Joyce Roetter, Karey Thorne, Kass Atkinson, Lee Cartwright, Melissa Pickett, Paul Chitwood, Paulette Marin, Rheanni Lightwater, Robert Waterman, Sam Berne, Sonia Masocco, Tom Brady, and Thomas Huebl.

My journey would not have even been possible without the love and support of Elaine Williams, my Spirit Sister.

For thirty years, her friendship was my bedrock; and I am eternally grateful to her.

Melissa Pickett, Lin Renner, and Dan McGuinness assisted me in the preparation of this manuscript for submission to Terra Nova Books. I am grateful to Marty and Scott Gerber of Terra Nova for publishing my book and to Mari Angulo and Art Tucker of Artotems Co. for their creative publicity.

Introduction

Wave Rider is a poetic reflection of my journey to heal from sexual abuse, abandonment, and neglect to wholeness of body, mind, and spirit. My journey has taken a lifetime. To use the metaphor of waves, sometimes the undertow nearly drowned me; but I survived. I hope this writing will be an inspiration to those who have also suffered greatly from abuse.

Growing up, I couldn't understand what was wrong with me. I was often alone, sad, and angry. Learning and comprehension were arduous. I felt as if I didn't fit in … in my family, in social groups, in my skin. My disastrous personal choices repeated and spiraled through the decades, and anxiety and depression were the hallmarks of my personality. Later, my diagnosis was determined to be post-traumatic stress disorder.

Two personal qualities saved me from implosion: my intelligence which allowed me to attain an education and my courage to go through the fire to discover my truth. My professional competence afforded me a living wage and the financial means to embark on psychotherapy and many modalities of alternative healing.

We have all been wounded, and what each of us does with those wounds is our healing path. This journey shuns victimization and embraces responsibility. Only I can heal myself by uncovering my layers hidden in darkness and integrating all that I am. For those of you just starting your healing process, be tenacious because no words can describe adequately the feeling of truly knowing yourself.

To paraphrase my poem "Karma," picking my parents was the beginning of always doing things the hard way. After my father deserted my mother and me, mother placed me in the care of an elderly couple who taught me to stand in the corner when I misbehaved. Then, before I was two, we went to live with my aunt, uncle, and three cousins. We were probably more than they bargained for. We stayed three years until my mother remarried.

My uncle sexually abused me beginning when I was two years young. I remember flying to the ceiling and looking down as I was being called. Being abused before I could talk changed everything, and I hovered outside my body for most of my life.

While blended family households are today's social norm, we were the exception in the early 1950s. I do not remember much of my childhood. I was the oldest, re-sponsible one, the little adult who was to be seen and not heard. Silence quickly turned to anger. I do remember being angry because what I was told by my mother did not match my experience. Years later, one exception was my mother's telling me that I was no longer welcome in my family's home. I never returned.

With no reason to stay, I headed west. My first stop was Michigan. I was fortunate to ride the wave of feminism in the 1970s, and my first career was in urban planning. Later, I earned my MBA. Those credentials eventually opened opportunities in health-care administration. While there were bumps and barriers in my professional life, I was proud of my accomplishments. However, my personal life was a disaster. After two brief failed marriages, I could no longer tolerate my emotional pain.

This pain and anxiety at the time were so severe I was nearly immobilized. From the depths of my frozen self, I slowly began to identify, peel back, and lay bare all of my layers of self-delusion. I had no idea who I was and no capacity to feel. I had negotiated my entire life through my mind. Later, I learned that this is how I survived.

The first section in this book is named "Darkness" and reveals my struggles, demons, and despair. As the years progressed and my self-awareness increased, I began to heal. "Between" captures the process of my multidimensional healing. In addition to western medicine, my healing therapies included acupuncture, chiropractic, massage, energy modalities, and medical intuition. With all that help, I realized that only I could heal myself.

"Spaciousness" begins with my arrival in Santa Fe, New Mexico. While my healing continues to this day, it is no longer all-consuming; and I have begun to actually live my life. I have given myself love and freedom and discovered my authentic spirit. In Santa Fe, I began writing poems and learned to sing. Today, my life is a blessing.

"Wave Rider" is my connection with the universe and the shifting paradigm that is movement toward the spirit of the divine feminine. Here, divine feminine refers to both women and men as we balance the feminine and the masculine in each of us. In America, the implosion of the old patriarchy is evident ubiquitously.

Writing the poems was part of my healing process, a vulnerable expression of my experience. In sharing these poems, I hope to provide some insight for others' journeys and a reminder that none of us is alone. The distance from frozen to free is long, difficult, and filled with peril—but essential to claim our authentic human spirit. There are no easy lessons, no free lunches or rides. In this time of change, our work is an inside job. With responsibility, determination, and courage, each of us can integrate all that we are and transform ourselves into who we want to be.

Darkness

Darkness came early. My mother was incapable of bonding with me, and there was no one to be her surrogate. Eventually, I became the sole reminder of her failed marriage and divorce at a time when divorce was the social exception. She and I composed our own karmic dance for the rest of her life.

Our going to live with my aunt, uncle, and cousins was a blessing which provided shelter, food, and a cat to play with. However, my consequential sexual abuse was too high a price. My memory of flying to the ceiling and looking down as I entered the bathroom where my uncle stood waiting was always vividly etched in my memory. However, I assumed that I had toddled into the bathroom by mistake. I could never figure out why he did not yell at me. (He had a very quick and mean temper.) It was not until I was fifty-eight years old that I understood that he was calling me, and I was his two-year-old prey. So for all those years, I did not know the source of my deep pain. All I wanted was peace.

The trauma of sexual abuse affected everything about my being. I think the most serious was the separation of thinking and feeling. When I first began psychotherapy, I remember being asked, "What do I feel?" I responded, "I don't feel anything." My brain had separated from itself. So I lived my life thinking . . . a desolate existence.

My inner self was nonexistent, and my emotional protection was armor. If I had been a man, I could have been a knight templar. My underbelly was a sea of anxiety, depression, and rage. When my overwhelming anxiety finally froze my very being, I could no longer tolerate my existence. I began my healing process at the age of forty.

Speaking Softly

I am not a poet.
Poetry requires
discipline
structure
writing within the lines.

I am a wise woman
who is weaving together
the threads of her life
who savors her
perspective
interconnectedness
every-woman-ness.

It is time to speak softly
so that the world hears.

Karma

I came into this world loaded with karma
karma to work on
karma to work through
karma to complete.
It is hard to imagine a newborn infant with all that
baggage.
I had picked my parents to facilitate this Earth work.
This was the beginning of always doing things the
hard way.

I have finally realized
that the walls I created to protect myself
were, in part, to protect me from my mother.
Together we did a karmic dance
one foot forward, three feet backward.
The floor was uneven and our steps collided.

Eventually I realized that
my actions, attributes, and attitudes replicated
the clinically depressed and sexually abused.
That felt like a lot.
Overwhelming is more precise.
The baggage nearly buried me.

Terror of Touch

Harshness, isolation, breathlessness
no bonding
just the empty space of a hospital crib
fingers intertwined
praying for love that never comes.

I stand in a black corner
waiting for a hug.
I stand in my crib crying
waiting for my mother who never comes.

A man does come who is cruel
wanting payment for my being alive.
His harsh invasion stops
my breath
my voice
my being.

I try the best I can
but living is so rage-filled
out of balance and misunderstood.
The black corner follows me everywhere.
There is no softness in the corner
no unconditional love
no cherishing.
At best I am a reminder of a mistake.
Things would be better without me.

How do I find my center in a lifeless black corner?
Without breath
without touch or love
I must take care of myself.
I wrap my mind and body in anxiety
just to breathe
just to survive.
But I can only do what I have been taught . . .

I learn to breathe so no one can hear.
I am still stuck in the black corner.
If I touch I cannot touch softly, lovingly.
There is no graceful flow
only harshness
toward myself
toward him, from him—Help.

Delusion

Family is a story
Family who loves me
Family who welcomes me into their home
Family who shares a heritage, a history
Family who lives a myth.

"You cannot come home. You cause too much trouble."
"Even people in your own family don't like you."
"I'm calling to make sure you are not coming
for Christmas."
"I have a meeting to go to; I cannot celebrate your
birthday."
"No, you cannot see her. She is dying."

The hurt comes from an expectation of kindness
too much to hope for in this lifetime.
Next time, I need to select my family for my heart
rather than from my need for lessons.
Perhaps then I can experience unconditional loving
belonging in safety
honoring my being.

Not in this lifetime.

Anxiety

This Earth walk is difficult for all human spirits.
I am so weary of having to be careful, judicious,
needing to protect myself from myself.
Incessant clatter inside and deafening noise outside
drown my spirit and leave a wasteland.
I am never sure where the limits are.
Some days the limits bind and paralyze.

Will I ever be free of anxiety in this lifetime?
My body remains encoded with trauma
ready to tear at my heart with the slightest shift.
I cry into the darkness of a broken child
knowing that old stories mold in boxes
of self-deception and myth-making.

Healing

I used to leave my body.
Then I taught myself how to stay in.
I think staying in is more painful.

My brain reviews all of the pain
in high definition, surround sound
which never ends.

My body is racked with stress
feeling as if it is going to explode
or implode.

I can't sleep, eat, feel safe.
I am super vigilant, hearing every noise
feeling out of control.

This Earth walk is difficult.
Someone else has inhabited my body
for so many decades.

Every once in a while now
he reemerges just as I am feeling safe.
All of my incredible sadness weighs on my heart.
I cry and cough and bring myself to the present
relieved and thankful for my healers.

Reality

He said "My father told me to do this, and
I loved him for it."

I can't imagine permission to be a child
or parents loving me
so that I could love them back.

My spirit has made difficult choices
in this lifetime . . .
parental abuse, neglect
emotional stifling, mental challenges.
I tell myself that I am improved
stamped like a box of detergent.
In reality I am still struggling.

I am exhausted from this lifetime.
My body tells the truth
can no longer hold the stress
and I collapse.

Getting Out of My Way

How can I live from my heart
when I can't get there?
My teacher says, "Drop down"
but my head still spins.

My throat is blocked.
What is in there?
First on the right side
then on the left
what is in there?

What can I not say to myself?
What am I holding onto
that I don't need any more?
My old self . . .
patterns, control, endless head chatter

If I let go of my old self
I can speak my truth
I can listen from my heart
I can live in my core.

If I let go of my old self
I can be.

Doorway

The woman walked through the doorway.
The doctor looked through the keyhole
of his training, prejudice, and experience
and didn't see her.
He didn't touch her, only looked
and concluded that she was old.

How does she force him to see her?
She can't.
She can only walk through the doorway
on her way to the other side.

Electronic Self

I find electronics offensive
occasionally convenient
mostly divisive
dividing my hello
from another's ability to hear.

To connect with another
you must show up, be present and open.
You cannot be open
when you are wired shut.

Between

I began psychotherapy after my second failed marriage. "One failed marriage could be his fault. Two are your responsibility." My body felt cold as ice and filled with fear. I talked for five years. Finally, my psychologist said, "Something happened to you before you could speak. I don't think it is to your benefit to discover what it was." It was time for a new therapist and a new city.

Life is not linear, literal, or three-dimensional. I just did the best I could. Psychotherapy began again after I collapsed in sobs during a meditation class, and I had no idea why. Healing is a spiral. When I finally broke through and discovered an "aha" insight, I was grateful until the next downward spiral. I maintained an external balance by keeping constantly busy. Life was exhausting. My psychologist suggested that body work would facilitate my healing, and my commitment to alternative therapies began.

I "jumped" when touched. I cried from a depth I did not know existed. Healing was about the courage to walk through the fire of my being to understand who I was and was not. My self-deception was appalling. When I was at my most desperate, I scheduled a healing therapy every day. Those times occurred both after my husband's sudden and unexpected death and two years later when I learned the full scope of my sexual abuse. Both times, I was clearly in crisis.

I built a labyrinth in the front meadow. This classical labyrinth truly saved my life by anchoring me to the earth. The design was completed just a few days before my abuse discovery. During that winter, I walked to the center of the labyrinth to save my soul and walked out to put myself back together. Then spring came.

Between

The space between
is the time and place of creation.

To experience the void
we must be still so that we hear our hearts.

We must quiet our busyness
unplug our ears
escape relentless noise

breathe

and find the space between.

Breakdown Breakthrough

I observed my mind's breakdown . . .
the start and stop of thoughts
the disconnection, the paralysis.
The brokenness of my spirit manifested
in my shallow breath and exhausted body.
I have broken down for lifetimes, and
my body has retained a memory of everything.
Cycles repeated themselves . . .
all the mistakes, poor choices, and clinging to delusion.
My body was fatigued and my spirit forfeited.

I declared that I would heal myself.
I threw it all into the fire and willed my breakthrough.
I broke down everything I have ever known
transforming myself by compassion and courage.
I honored my strength and intention and
recognized the universal in my finite being.
Breakthrough demanded individual responsibility,
consciousness, and spirit.
May these attributes hold the center for the New Earth.

Silence

Incessant clatter and deafening activity
drowned me in anxiety and depression.
I cried into the darkness of the broken child
in fear; my spirit wasted.

Years of facing my own fire
years of peeling away my soul
and I am done . . .
confronting, analyzing, synthesizing
trying to make sense of the dark.

Finally
the light and silence, blessed silence . . .
Nothing had prepared me for
this quiet divinity.
My body echoes silence.
My spirit knows silence.
I walk in silence
and smile in gratitude for
my healers and teachers and
myself.

Be Here Now

I write because no one is here to listen.
I write when I don't want to forget.
I write when my mind spins.

The stars and planets are aligned
forecasting great changes.
I am here to create equilibrium of
feminine and masculine
Earth and sky
silence and sound
light and dark
peace and peace.

To do this, I must expand my spirit
into the universe
and expand my senses
to know my divinity.
Then my mind will quiet and my heart will open.

Body Talk

My body speaks to me with a loud voice.
She tells me the truth of my thoughts
and the rightness of my actions.
I need only to listen.
She brings up the haunting past
in this lifetime or others.

My body is an historian.
My brain never pauses, can't be still.
My back constricts; my shoulders harden.
My breathing is fast and shallow.
My body has its own memory of everything.

Only by identifying and working through
all my painful history can I release the memories
which ensnare me in the past and interfere with
my presence.
Only after the work does my brain quiet
my back relax and my breath deepen
into my interior peace.

Dancing on the
Edge of Death

When there is no breath
I spiral down into nothingness.
When there is no breath
passing to the other side is possible.

Love for myself needs to be
my center of discernment
making decisions for my highest good
slowing so that I can hear myself
being intentional to save my life.

I have burned my past.
Its ashes fly in the wind.
I am no longer encumbered with shadows
of lovelessness.

I can sing my joy
my voice and breath strong and defiant.
I will not need this lesson again
and I am grateful.

Student

I walk into class
a place, a space so familiar.
I have been here before
in this body, in this lifetime
to learn, to experience, to be.
But today is different.

The space I hold has expanded.
My energy has grounded
into the center of Mother Earth.
My feet connect with her heart.
My heart connects with everyone in the room.

Mine is an intentional journey of self-healing.
I feel a stillness that I have never known
a sense of comfort in my body.
The student is becoming the wise one
and I am joyful.

Surrender

Surrender to my softness
The pendulum swings in a wide clockwise affirmative.
The answer comes as easily as the clouds floating by.

I have struggled with such difficulty
my body exhausted
my mind exploding
my spirit desperate.

How difficult it seemed to pierce the impenetrable walls
protecting my heart
my sense of self
my betrayal.

Then I saw the clouds and
I took a breath and relaxed into my softness
a softness that I had never felt before
a softness surrounding my heart
opening my heart to my wholeness and beauty.

It is time to be.
I have no more energy or desire for doing.
I have done enough outside of myself.
It is time for my own creation.

Spaciousness

There is a sacred energy, a spirit of freedom in Santa Fe. The spaciousness of the blue skies, the beauty of the mountains, and the sense of oneness with the earth permeate everything. The Indian cultures remind us of the divinity of nature and our interconnection with all. Gratitude, not greed, is the ethos. When I visited Santa Fe, I had no intention of relocating. Then I found my home and moved in six weeks later. The magic had begun.

The healing community is vast, multidisciplinary, innovative, and extraordinarily competent. Each healer led to my next. The most significant healers for me were those specializing in post-traumatic stress disorder who wove my brain together energetically. Having the left and right sides of my brain connected created a new life.

I was blessed with access to an abundance of spiritual teachers and sacred sites. However, I was the master of my healing through both intention and learned skills. Accessing my own energy and the multidimensional energy surrounding me was essential for my journey. My spirit manifested fire in my belly and the courage to continue my process.

Openness and curiosity led to never-imagined possibilities. I gave myself permission to explore. I wrote my first poem during a women's circle. I was amazed that the women liked it, and I was amazed that I liked it. My poems became my storytelling. I also dared to learn to sing. From four years old, I had been told that I cannot sing. So I took lessons and now can sing "Happy Birthday" without mouthing the words. I don't know how my next creative venture will unfold. I am waiting to be surprised.

Coming to Santa Fe

You come to Santa Fe
to breathe the air
to see the beauty
to come alive.

You come to Santa Fe because you must.
Your spirit calls, a spirit you have never heard before
but you know she is true.
You come to Santa Fe for
the earth, colors, beauty, wind.

You come to Santa Fe to save your soul from
mediocrity, hypocrisy, materialism, soul-less-ness.
You come to Santa Fe so that you can be
genuine, congruent, truth-filled, happy, and alive.

You come to Santa Fe to be a part a community
loving the land, loving to laugh
determined to be our essential selves
strong and caring
committed to the Earth
committed to our journeys
committed to each other in a circle
a circle that is changing the world.

Singing Lessons

Since kindergarten I was told that I cannot sing . . .
singing that is socially acceptable or tolerable
singing on tune.
So I shut my mouth, hummed to myself, and
said, "I can't sing."
And for decades I didn't.

Singing requires attention, breath and an open mouth
that resonates with sounds from the heart.
Singing is a melody of connectedness within and
with the spirit of others.
Singing is universal.

The first time you heard my voice,
you were willing to be my teacher and
help me slay the dragon of my musical myth.
I practiced exercises
breathed deeply
expanded my vocal range
distinguished sounds of vowels and
began to sing.

I am grateful for your encouragement
a gift of spirit, heart, and generosity.
I did slay the dragon of silence
and now I sing.

Gift of Love

The gift of unconditional love to ourselves is soulful.
Discovering who we are is hard work
requiring truth and strength.
We descend through the dark night of the soul.
Along the way our vulnerabilities and frailties
overpower our core.

Loving ourselves is an unpeeling of layers
to find our integrity, authenticity and congruence
to find our wholeness.
We pluck the strings of the harp
dance in time with the wind and
create music of the soul, a love song.

Then our heart beats with the metronome
in never-ending rhythm encircling two.
The grace of unconditional love for another
plays in the heavens and
echoes in the waves for eternity.

Circle of Women

How powerful to be an elder
walking the land
connecting with our souls
being present for each other
birthing the New Earth.

The alchemy is for us to create
beauty, wisdom, healing, and peace from the chaos.
We have come with knowing in our eyes
truth in our hearts and
congruence in our souls.
We are the ones we have been waiting for.
We welcome new and old friends into the circle
which is large enough to hold all of us.
We dance and sing in gratitude and grace.

We are changing the world.

Woman Made of Fire

Her eyes dance with fire.
Her laugh taunts the gods.
Her wisdom follows spirit.
Her hands create magic.

She breaks the rules and makes her own
knowing that the wisdom, strength and
frailty of her ancestors
spiral in her consciousness and
splash in oil on linen.
She creates from the depths of her experience
in this world and others.

Light emanates from her center into the four directions.
The flow of her vitality fills all space.
There is nothing timid here.
The fierceness and fire burn into
creativity, vibrancy, and radiance.
Her blood and passions flow.
Her colors pierce our hearts, transfix our souls and
make us believers in Earthly transcendence.
Her sense of balance, myth, and magic
transport us to another place and time
as she burns her way to her destiny.

When the Portal Opens

When the portal opens, the universe is white.
The brilliance encompasses all
the galaxies, stars, Earth, me.
The heart connection is palpable.
There is no beginning, no end, no separation.

Knowing that I am one with the stars shifts
my perception of everything.
I feel different, expansive and vibrating.
Perhaps this is how the Earth feels right now
expansive and vibrating
waiting for the next white light

Teaching My Spirit to Fly

I am standing on a cliff.
I jump and disappear into the clouds.
My wings spread and I fly effortlessly
and joyfully.

This dream is empowering
a dream of life
that I create from the fire in my belly.

You cannot be afraid or timid if you want to fly.
Fearlessness and courage support your wings.
Determination and tenacity stoke your spirit.
Clarity of purpose hones your vision.

No one can fly for you
and no one can prevent you from flying.
Flying is an inside job.
Flying is a metaphor for living your life.
When you teach your spirit to fly
you are free.

Meadow

It is a goddess day.
Her moisture surrounds me
as I stand at the edge of the meadow of purple and red
flowers.
The fragrance of roses dances in the wind.
The presence of the goddess envelops me
like a warm, soft shawl.

Today I know that there is no going back.
The mists between the worlds are thin and
the light of the meadow draws me in.

In this new place
I am authentic, present, and peaceful.
Only purple and red flowers belong here.
All else is left behind.
The old energy cannot survive in the meadow.

The feminine energy of the goddess is reemerging
as we dance in a circle radiating light.

Surprise

This morning my heart spoke.
"It is time to write."
It is a time of change, surprise
life threatening, life affirming
life endings, life beginnings
purging old, embracing new.
This seems like duality.
It is not.

The present is the web of
interconnectedness, wholeness, oneness, knowingness.
Breath, thoughts, heart-space affect the web
subtly, profoundly, powerfully.
There is no beginning and no end.
Birth, life, death, rebirth
the circle of beingness continues
and interweaves the energies of the web.

My work on this Earth-plane is to intend
peace, wholeness, freedom.
My work on this Earth-plane is to honor
earth, air, fire, and water.
My work on this Earth-plane is to be present
in a spiritual circle that is surprising the world
and even ourselves.

Eclipse

The solar eclipse had begun.
The clouds danced before the sun, then parted
so that we could witness a cosmic event
the union of sun and moon.
The energy is now.

We had all been guessing
that the energy of the divine feminine
was spiraling in.
We are no longer guessing.
The shift is now.

We were born for this time
to help shift the universe
to dismiss the past
to live now.
Everything is different.
Nothing is the same
except the sun and moon.

Free

In the fullness of the moon
I recognize that I have set myself free . . .
free from my old assumptions and behaviors
free to choose how I want to be.

This is the shift I have been waiting for
yet could never imagine
describing the moon with no sight
finding my center of grace
knowing gratitude and awe.

My voice is powerful and on pitch.
My words resonate to the universe.
"I am free."

Sun and Stars

The sun dropped below the horizon
engulfing me in darkness.
The journey is difficult,
and the darkness has lasted a lifetime.
My resiliency wears close to the edge
of the mists.
My spirit guide pointed to my path of
"education, inspiration, and enlightenment."
The potential is close.
I need only wait for the wheel to turn
and be ready to swing on a star.

Playbook

Twist the lens, change the sight
Everything is play, everything is light

I am my own kaleidoscope
With colors going round
Different shapes and sizes
And mystery to be found

I can laugh, I can play
I can choose to be present
I can look through any prism
And find my effervescence

This is the time for an open heart
I don't have to dig deep
I only have to start

With polka dots flying from my coat
Striped pants billowing in the wind
With high-top sneakers on my feet
And a hat upon my head
I am ready to greet the quantum
As my teacher said

Wave Rider

The energy is changing. The duality of the old patriarchy is crumbling. The truths and lies of institutions are being revealed. But institutions are not abstract constructs. Individuals participate in and give permission for the collective. This is a time of chaos and opportunity; focusing on the negative will only keep us there. Envisioning the oneness and potential of humanity will create that future.

These turbulent times of shifting planets, an erupting Earth, and personal challenges require us to be grounded, centered, and in our bodies. Just withstanding the energetic chaos is an accomplishment. Our core strength and authenticity enable us to survive. To give our power away to anyone or anything outside of ourselves weakens our spirit and capacity to thrive.

We have all signed up to be here now, to ride the waves of the New Earth. Our choices affect everything. Judgment, fear, and anger are pervasive. To understand that energy attracts like energy, we only need to observe our political morass. Ours is a culture of blaming others for our faults. However, we are responsible for who we are.

So if we desire to live in a world of peace, we must create that within. Then peaceful energy will attract others who are and intend to be peaceful. It is time to create who we want to be. To change the world, we must change ourselves. The time is now.

Wave Rider

I ride the crest of the wave of the New Earth.
The waters of Gaia are her blood
and I taste her sacrament.

I ride the wave of my own re-creation
challenging my assumptions and beliefs of who I am.
My rote behavior and automatic responses
transform into reflection and new choices.
My spirit knows freedom.

I am not who I have been.
I don't know who I will be
other than the wave rider
alive, on the edge
of the New Earth.

Poem

She said, "It is a wonderful poem."
"It saved my life."
"It is about my journey too."

Another's words capture our hearts
and the core of our experience.
How can that be?

Perhaps we are all on the same journey.
Perhaps we are all connected
simply seeking freedom and peace.
Along the way we waste a lot of ourselves
with busyness, worry, and minutiae.

When we discover that we are the emperor with no robe,
then we can sit in stillness
read a poem about ourselves
and change everything.

Smallness

Narrow ruts of perception
distort our ability to navigate in our infinite universe.
A singular idea embeds in our understanding
and prohibits recognition or the possibility
of other alternatives.

So we find others like us,
who speak our language,
share ethnicity, culture, traditions
and preferences for divinity and social norms.
Then we become a herd comfortable with our own.
Our smallness is fortified, and we think we are reality.

Being small breeds righteousness, fear, and
entrenchment.
Any understanding of the interconnectedness of the
universe
collapses into intolerance and finally violence and war.
Perhaps this is what we are witnessing in the world . . .
a lot of small people
with singular ideas
ignoring the universe.

Flying Metaphors

This is a time of flying metaphors and wisdom
personal and intimate, global and expansive.
While the energy is shifting, our bodies
keep us in the density of Earth.
Our bodies may be the first or last to show up
but never wrong.
We must define the discomfort
with deep, personal honesty
naming our essence and truth.

Being on a spiritual path is a journey within
not to any external destination, belief, or power.
When we know our divine essence
the debris of eternity peels away, and
we focus with precision on our core.
Clarity creates health, wholeness and light
and takes a lifetime.

Nature Distilled

Holding the tension between opposites
is a life skill that keeps us on the edge.
Perhaps the edge is where the universe is
so much change, too much change.

We are recreating ourselves . . .
the tension, the energy, the colors, the void.
All we know is that we are here now
feeling and holding the tension.

Our being grounded and centered transmutes the energy
into something tangible, life affirming.
There is a quietness.
We are here to be alchemists
mixing the dark and the light
holding the tension
recreating creation.

Awareness

The Earth shakes.
We are between the worlds
of patriarchy and the divine feminine.
The hierarchy, control, and separateness
knock us over as we reach
for new and unfamiliar ways.

Our DNA is embedded with all we have done.
Breaking old patterns is our challenge.
We dance between
who we have been and who we intend to be.
Consciousness is awareness of our contradictions.
We have much work to be.

So we sit quietly in silence until
a prayer blesses those of us who are gathered
to greet the divine feminine and
proclaim our oneness, peacefulness,
and heart-centeredness.
We have much work to be peace.

Teacher

If we are conscious on this Earth plane,
the work we do is soul work.
It is hard work.
Sometimes we have to repeat and repeat
the same work
from the same lesson.
A patient teacher is required.

Our teacher is an alchemist turning pain into light.
The wisdom of the ages has settled in her.
She speaks from the center of her open heart.
She is present for herself and all of us
drawing us in so that we can be free.

When we find a teacher who sets us free,
we can transform ourselves
and move on to our next lesson.
Then there are no words for our gratitude
only our spirits shining back.

Ceremony

The moon melts through the mists
and the stones stand tall.
The quiet of the night envelops us
and we are transported
to another time
to another life
to our true essence.

We have been here before among the mists and stones.
We have been here before in ceremony and song.
We have been here before, and we have come home
to heal the Earth
to heal the stones
to heal ourselves.

Ours is a pilgrimage of spirit and courage.
With expansion of heart and clarity of purpose
we welcome the divine feminine.
Standing in this circle, we know that she has changed us
and we are grateful.

Our new journeys begin now.

Now the Veil Is Thin

The veil is thin between the worlds.
We are both individuals and community
connected with our hearts
connected with each other in a circle.
The cone of energy is a powerful vortex into the universe
to the other side.
We will be there soon . . . to the other side
when we have finished our work in this lifetime.
Do we ever know what that work is?
Do we ever know when it is complete?

As we honor those who have passed,
we honor that part of them that is in us
that part of them that we will pass on to the next
generations.
When the veil is thin between the worlds,
one cannot be too literal.
Nothing is separate.
We are all connected.
We are all connected to Mother Earth.
It is Mother Earth who nourishes our lives
and collects our dust.
Now the veil is thin and we are one.

Wild Women

Buttercups and Queen Anne's lace
line the path of a thousand years.
We walk back into our consciousness.
We walk back into the mystery and the mists.
We walk into our greatness and power.

Our hearts are open, expansive, deep, and wise.
Our connection with the sacredness of the Earth
whirls in the wind and sets us free.
The moon and the sun balance the energies of the
ancient ones
with the possibilities of our future.

We are spirals dancing toward the unimaginable
in grace, peace, and centeredness.
We are today's priestesses and tomorrow's wise women.
We hold the mysteries, the star dust, and the rain.
We laugh from our bellies.
We dance from our innate sense of our feet
being one with the Earth.

We are wild women, noble and timeless.

Messages and Miracles

We are all connected
as we break old patterns and
dance between who we have been
and who we intend to be.
We are the muses telling our stories,
passing along heritage and
giving a context for the now.

We need context to understand
the universal cycles and truths
the memories that flow between us
as we sing our strength.

We swim in the colors of earth and water and
gather the mystery in our bones and blood.
We are Mother Earth's caretakers.
Messages are hidden in plants and streams.
The stones whisper to us
and we whisper to the stones.
We gather to share our magic
as we burst into beauty.

Prophesy

She had to wait to be free
of contracts, demons, and darkness.
The spiral dance released the karma
and light flowed into her life.

Her spiritual journey is before her.
It is hers to choose.
It is hers to serve.
Unknown possibilities await
when the wheel turns.

Core strength brought her here, to now.
Anything is possible in the new energy
on the New Earth.
The prophesy of "educate, inspire, and enlighten"
will unfold in this new era.

She has chosen to be here
to do the work
to bring in light and love in her unique way.
This time, the journey
will create synchronicity within her
and heaven on Earth.

Women of Now

The veil is lifting.
Our collective unconscious emerges from the desert
as the moon rises over the mountains.
We are the hearts, voices, and knowing of the ancient ones.
We are the truth-sayers for those who are coming.

We can be silent no longer.
Our deep wisdom is everywhere
in the symbols and colors and depth of life.
We carry the waters that transform
darkness into light.
We are the alchemists.

We are the women of now.
The cycle of stones, moon, and blood
is just beginning.
We move all of the energies into peace,
mystery, and oneness.

We are the new warriors of truth and power.
Our spirits shine through the weight of the ages.
We breathe and know from our
hearts, intuition, and essence.
Welcome the divine feminine in all of us.

About the Author

Rebecca Pott Fitton explored different places and professional work. She grew up in Delaware and went to college in upstate New York. After graduating from Keuka College, she earned an M.A. in international relations at the University of Delaware. Then she headed to Michigan for careers in urban planning and health-care administration and an MBA from the University of Detroit. She continued working in health care in Ohio and retired as president of CareView Home Health in Middletown, Ohio.

Retirement can be a busy time. Fitton brought her business acumen to service on five nonprofit boards. After her husband, Richard, died, she realized that the time had come to remake herself. As the lyrics of the song go, "I'd built a life wrapped so tight it was strangling me." Freedom was a spirit call from Santa Fe, New Mexico.

Fitton arrived in Santa Fe in 2008 and fell in love with the blue skies, clean mountain air, a vibrant community, and the arts. Her first poem was written under a juniper tree.

Readers can follow Fitton's continuing journey on her blog at www.RebeccaPottFitton.com.